PLIGHT

Flight of the BUTTERFLY

IS IT THE END FOR OUR WING-ED FRIENDS?

Don G. Ford

FREE BOOKMARK FOR MY READERS!!!

Flying from flower to flower and book to book

THIS BOOK IS DEDICATED
To my sweet daughter and fishing buddy

[Picture taken by Janice Huse in Georgia]

"Dad that butterfly keeps circling you over and over!"

One of many true stories I share about family life

Stories in my Library

Gone Fishin'

by Don Ford

Author Notes:

I am a storyteller from the word go. Some of it is real and some of it is imagined. My goal is to entertain, maybe turn a few smiles right side up. An artist from my youth, I write and paint in different colors. Cheers.

P.S. Watch for the butterfly in our story

Now don't everyone get all touchy feelie on me, and I will share what happened just this morning.

"Dad, are we going fishing today?" My daughter had been anticipating this for some time.

She began by relating to me that she could not sleep the night before. She woke up at 5 am, 6 am, 6:30 am, and here we were talking at 7 am.

"Yes, honey. I promised you, if it weren't raining, that we would hit the water."

"Do you want me to get dressed right now?" She was more than excited.

"Sure babe, go ahead. Don't wear your good shoes."

For the last three years, I had taken my girl fishing. Now at 11, she still wants to go, but will still not chance putting the worm on the hook.

To my sweet daughter and fishing buddy

When we arrived at Jamesville Beach, the questions began. "Are we too early for the fish?" This question followed on the heels of, "Why do they take so long to bite?"

"We are here to learn first how to fish, and to also learn to be patient. So start with talking to me in a whisper, since they can hear us. Unless they are starving, they will eat when they feel like it."

"Dad, does the worm feel it when it goes on the hook? Does it hurt them?"

"You notice how careful I am, and I don't do it too fast. Maybe if I were too quick and rough it might hurt."

I was hoping the questions wouldn't get any harder to answer.

[A cover picture I created for TONI,

one of my book clients in Virginia.]

This is a cool book of a mother remembering all those earlier kid years. The art is done by her grand children. ENJOY a look at it.

https://tsw.createspace.com/title/4802392

HIGH FLYING TALES - A KITE NAMED JACK.

GONE FISHIN'

"Dad, that butterfly keeps circling you over and over. Do you know what that means?"

"No, honey, but I bet you are going to tell me, aren't you?."

"That's right, I am. It means you are a gentle person. That's what my teacher told us in science class."

Later, I noticed the butterfly let me pick it up with my fingers. Shortly after this, a dragonfly landed on my shoulder, and my daughter said, "Hey, he likes you too, Dad."

But she remembers my infamous dragonfly story that I sold to a magazine, where a lone dragonfly saved me from hoards of black-flies.

See Dragonfly Story here >>>

My Best Friend and HERO by Don Ford

A story I love to tell over and over is the one about The Lone Stranger. He was beautiful and perfect in every way. On a special day in my life he came to my rescue. At a time when I was being physically attacked, and there was not another soul around, he appeared on the scene. No, he wasn't a Knight in shining armor, and he didn't arrive on a white horse, either.

He came quite frankly on a wing and a prayer. He was just what I hoped for, dreamed of, and absolutely needed at the time. He also came at just the precise moment when I was under siege. No one else would have fit the bill; the perfect answer to my dilemma.

This tale goes back a number of years, but every detail is etched in my heart and brain. Every point in my story is absolutely true. I could never have been more thankful for a friend than at that time. Much of my life is found out in the vastness of nature; a very curious place to work.

Did I see it coming? No. I had no clue I would be barraged by hundreds of black flies. These tiny, almost invisible creatures from the dark domain, showed up at a very unwelcome time.

They couldn't just show up one at a time, but had to bring all their evil friends and relatives with them. Most are out for blood, and on the day of this incident, they probably exacted a gallon of mine - along with a pound of flesh.

The home I was landscaping was situated out in the country with no other houses in sight. It was a lovely new home in need of lots of plantings to really set it off. A flower garden full of perennials was slated to go into the front. All of the other shrubs and trees were in place when it happened.

I began work on the flower garden, and those creatures that were lying in wait decided to make their move. There was no escaping the next few minutes as all of those little black devils came pouring in on me. I felt them before I actually saw them. Like a gang of miners, they went to work hammering and drilling me.

Back in a corner of the lot was my hero. He was watching, I am sure, and waiting to make his move. Like a Blue Angel, this iridescent friend came swooping to my rescue. It wasn't two minutes before he had the situation well in hand, and had thwarted or eaten every pesky black fly that was in my face. I stood frozen in amazement as my best friend of all time zipped in and out around my head, face, and neck. This was obviously a picnic for him, but the end of a nightmare for me.

The 'masked man' who rescued me was none other than the lone dragonfly; the only helper I needed that day. Highlighted in a magazine story with Angels on Earth, and two million readers, he made a big splash with the garden folks out there. Now in the Spring (May/June 2011 issue) another rescue story was told. Watch for it to highlight more heroes,

this time in my vegetable garden; "The Plot Against Me".
[Siamese Angels]

Back to our original fishing story >>>

During today's little adventure we both caught a fish. This year was different; this year my fish and her fish were the same size. Other years she always caught the biggest fish. That of course remains our little secret; now doesn't it?

Today we only fished for a little over an hour and then headed home. By the time we got back, Mom was waiting to hear the tall tales.

"Mom, guess what? Dad exaggerated today. He said the fish we saw in the water was as big as a house."

"Show me how big it was." Then my daughter proceeded to stretch her hands as far apart as she could. "Wow, it sounds like your dad wasn't too far off."

Author Notes: There are moments in our lives that we hold on to dearly, this will always be one of those times, along with countless others.

Comes a Friend

By Don G. Ford

Strolling down the pebbled beach
In the early morning light
Noiseless, quiet all around
Not a single friend in sight

Except for gentle splashings
Of waves that lap the shore
Not much sound was heard this day
Midst tufts of grass - stones galore

Suddenly a friend stops by
To share her time, it's true
Her colors catch me by surprise
First she lands upon my shoe

Then I reached out toward her
Butterflies don't make a sound
Cruising by me, she did fly
Made a circle all around

Next she landed on my hand
Stayed a while and then she flew
Fluttered past me then was gone
This friend - she chased away my blues

My editor notes read: This poem was produced with a friend in mind. The gentleman had just lost his wife three months before. He was having a difficult time adjusting. I wrote this specifically for him. His wife was a great lover of butterflies; so I thought this poem was fitting. The butterfly is HER. He loved it, and he hung it on his outside door for all to view. I produced it in 11x17 card stock, and it was perfect for the door. Cheers. Don

ANOTHER BUTTERFLY :-}

A FISH IN WATER - DOING THE BUTTERFLY!!!

Even if all the butterflies go the way of the dinosaur, I'll always have this picture of my daughter, Erin, to remember them by. Will they also have to rename this competition swim stroke? I certainly hope they never do!

*

Have you noticed, kids are getting smarter?

A chapter in the book *Musings to Amuse*

Frog and the Butterfly

by Don G. Ford

Some friends to Clay Pond arrived in pairs.

Freddie and Thad were friends from another pond.

This would be their new and permanent home.

Clay Pond

Freddie The Frog & Thaddeus Toad

Don G. Ford

Catch this book too on Amazon by Don G. Ford

"Marge, why is this kid's story book on my side of the table?" Jon picked up the book to show her. "It's full of pictures of butterflies and pond life."

"Oh, that is Evie's new library book. I wanted to show you that your little third grader is now reading at a fifth grade level. Isn't that wonderful?"

"What do you want; look at who she has as parents." Jon thumbed the pages.

"Guess what, I'd be turning the pages too. Look at all of the graphics."

"Jon, take the time to read a little of it. It is too advanced for third grade. Give your daughter a bit of credit here."

Marge turned to go.

"Look Marge, I meant nothing by that. You have to admit it has a lot of pictures." Jon tried to salvage his ego.

"Hi Evie, we were just checking out your new book from the library at school. Cool pictures, huh?" Jon spoke first.

"Are you kidding; I thought the pictures were overdone. It gives it a cluttered look. And the pictures do nothing to help the story, except add lots of color." Evie waited to hear their comments.

"By the way Evie, your dad was just saying he thought it had a lot of pictures, maybe a few too many." Mom gave Jon the benefit of the doubt.

"Next time I go to the library, I am going to see if this writer has any more books out, hopefully they will be a little wordier. Susan Frank is a good storyteller, and she gives me ideas for some things I want to write about. And someday I want to follow in her shoes as a published author. I like the addition of poetry in her book too - it adds a fresh new look to her writing." Evie quietly slipped out of the kitchen with those thoughts still hanging in the air.

"Marge, are you sure she's our daughter? I know we are both college grads, but at 6 years of age, I was not that smart, and could not express myself that well." Jon stood looking puzzled.

"Do me a favor and speak for yourself. She is definitely Olsen stock, like my mother before me. She is for sure her mother's daughter." Then Marge promptly left the kitchen as well.

Note:
Whose kid is it this time, when they are so smart?
Children are doing things at earlier ages. They start them on computers in grade school. (V-Tech.) Now we have to ask them for advice, since they are so computer savy; at least I know I do.

[The butterfly bush, true to its name, is a favorite of butterflies as well as bees and other pollinators.]

Butterfly bushes are a favorite among many gardeners. The showy, fragrant blooms <u>attract all sorts of beneficial insects to your garden</u>. You may even find a hummingbird or two stopping by to enjoy the nectar inside the tiny flowers.

Many times we are held captive by life's events.

In This Prison Place by Don G. Ford
Thank you for the great butterfly picture, MissGdRnch

It's so cold here midst the darkened walls
My movements are but a stirring and no more
No lifting of my legs or arms to stretch
Pressed in on all sides by hopelessness

How cruel to leave me here in this place
My numbness I am feeling all about my sides
The ache and cruel mocking seems absurd
When will my time be up and I'm set free?

I've lost all conscientiousness of time
No one seems to even care at all for me
The walls are now all closing in on me
I've all but given up; I can not fight

At last, a shaft of light has found its way
Through thickened wall of dirt or maybe clay
The long dark night of my imprisonment
Could not destroy my own desire to live

The door is open wide and I will flee
The stars hold much in store for me
Or I will fly to distant galaxies above
As I gaze upon each one in ecstasy

Author Notes:

I have recently left a position that held me prisoner for 5 years. Today I am shed of it. It is a warm and comforting feeling. Not the fact that I do not have work at this present time, but that the lie I lived is over and I am free to pursue truth if I so desire. Many feel trapped by their circumstances, and death should never form an option. Never, ever give up, but hold on until the door is unlatched or the light comes streaming through, which you have not seen for months or even years. Wait for it; it will come. This was set up as free flowing lines to express the elements of life that were closing in on me, it seemed. Cheers.

I so remember my first day of classes at Paul Smith's College. (Fall of 1967) Even though Gabriel's Campus was where many Forestry and Surveying students lived, it was where most of our classes were held also. We seldom ventured onto the main campus. I never really figured out the formula of who lived and attended classes where. I think most of the 2 year Terminal Forestry students were housed here, or at White Pine Camp, but don't quote me. Those going on to four year schools were usually on main campus. They were called Pre-Professionals.

It was time to fill out our first paperwork in a certain LOCKED classroom at Gabriel's Campus. I can only describe my first teacher as a real NUTS and BOLTS kind of guy. Professor Gould Hoyt was not letting a locked door stand in his way. He turned his back to the door, muttered words I can't share here, and Boom he took the door out with his butt. We were then able to quietly seat ourselves, and fill out the necessary paper work. We all knew this was a teacher we wanted to pay strict attention to, and it turns out he really was, and we really did. He didn't care too much for the facilities at Gabriels, but he taught us just the same. It wasn't personal; I think he just wanted to do his teaching mostly on main campus.

P.S. My love of nature and the environment started here, at the School of the Adirondack's. LOVE THAT NAME!!! I went on from here to work in State Forestry, and I also taught Landscaping Classes all across the State of New York for the next 30 years!

Her Name is Iris

By Don Ford

Iris has a tale to tell,
Her story will unfold.
A bold and elegant display,
Her colors, petals – we behold.

Perchance the sun is out today.
It adds some warmth, a smile.
Though Iris faces are short lived,
A grand appearance for a while.

And gazing we are carried off,
These mesmerizing flowers;
They know that they are being watched,
By each of us for untold hours.

Most of my classes were at the max. (15), with some adult learners on a waiting list for the next class. I think I did Prof. Hoyt proud, and he's smiling down from some 'lofty mountain grandeur'. To me he will always be synonymous with the name of Forestry. https://www.createspace.com/4429444

I'll now share a story about MOTHS, since they are probably cousins to the butterfly. :-}

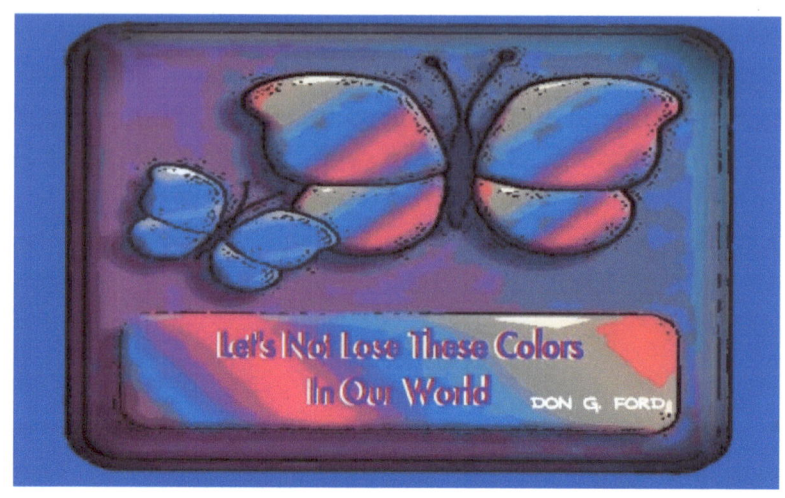

One Mad Moth Speaks Out

Published on July 27, 2017

[Don Greywolf Ford](#) **I'll leave you all with a thought regarding a Moth Hunt. I've been on this trek for real. What we never see in our world are these gorgeous other flyers who come out mostly at night. Maybe more true believers will join me on my next adventure. This time for real. Cheers, Don**

One Mad Moth Speaks Out

[I love writing fiction pieces, and giving voices to those who could never speak for themselves, except providing they are endowed with special powers, like a writer's pen, which brings them to life. Cheers, Don]

Our Fun Tale Begins...

I ventured out one night to try and capture unusual moths in their evening environment. I took along my trusty flashlight, my canister of rotting fruit to get their attention, and a jar with a lid to capture them in. I do this at night so no one will see me and laugh. Actually

I go out after dark because that's when they are the most active.

The strong odor from the fruit is too temping for them. The real secret is to use a small brush and swipe the gooey fruit on trees in your yard. Now give the fruit a chance to do its job. Wait for at least a half an hour, before returning to inspect those earlier trees. Lo and behold there they are.

The very first time I went on a moth hunt, I was shocked at the numbers and varieties of these hidden creatures of the night. I'm guessing the strong light of day drives them into hiding. Butterflies flutter during the day and probably enjoy basking in the Sun as they move from flower to flower.

This one night there was a different feel in the air. I sensed I was not alone. After returning to a tree to check its moth population, only one of them appeared. At this point, those of you reading my tale who don't believe nature can communicate with humans, please go no further. Only true believers need to follow on with my story.

You see, this one lone moth spoke up quite clearly, and was fluent in English.

"I am angry with all of you."

"Are you talking to me?

"No, not you in particular. You at least give us the time of day in our evening flights."

"Why are you mad, and is it only you that feel this way?"

"I'm the spokesman for all of my kind, dispelling myths about us moths."

"Do tell!

(Our story continues on from this point with our Moth speaking up!)

"Our bravest among us have ventured forth into the day to try and find those humans who would pay attention to us. We are not as beautiful as your butterfly friends, but we have our own stories to tell!"

"Why speak to me?"

"Because you were brave enough to venture into our world of nighttime surprises. Yes, the day holds its own charms, but the evening is full of fun and frolic as well. Moths enjoy playing games and chasing each other from tree to tree. You probably hadn't noticed there are thousands of different moths who live near your home."

"I'm only just now learning. Some are quite magnificent. You in particular are quite beautiful, with your hidden bright blue hues under your wings."

"We are called just that; Underwings. We come in a rainbow of colors. You are only seeing a small glimpse of our world."

"Why tell me this?"

"I've seen you during the day, and I like what I've noticed about you. You are a gentle soul, and wouldn't hurt a flea. I've seen you sweep up tiny ants and spiders, taking them back outdoors where they belong."

"They aren't hurting anyone, they just got lost, and I take them back to where they came from."

"Now you know why I chose to speak to you . I had to vent with someone in your world to let them know I'm angry that they ignore all of us. We have feelings too. I want to scream, look at us, we should count for something in this world."

"I'll certainly pass your message around, and find more true believers among all of the humans. I'm sure thousands of our kind would be thrilled to learn of your activities, since there are so many of you."

WHERE EAGLES FLY

As the name implies, Don writes with a down-home flavor. Nature and conservation are popular topics with him. He writes in many genres. He is known for his poetry and story telling. Short stories are his favorite form of writing. To date he has sold numerous short stories to magazines across the U.S. Most have their roots in nature - of course. Recently he was invited to be his town's Poet Laureate. The mayor tild him he could think about it, to which he replied: "What's to think about, I'm there."

Much of his poetry and writing is accompanied by art work. He claims it helps to tell his stories better.

Random musings everywhere
But I won't let them stop me
I like what's concrete, set in stone
Not those fleeting gestures

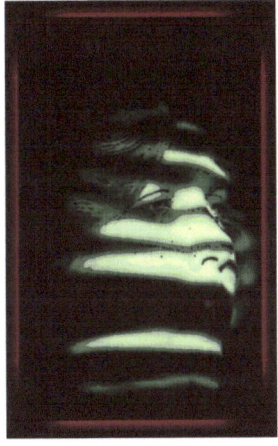

Let what we say have meaning
Say what we must, then move along
Nothing wrong with sharing thoughts
Don't be afraid - speak your mind

Let no one bully you about
Putting words into your mouth
Be your own person when you share
What's in your heart - let it out

Time to be both flesh and blood
No longer hiding in the shadows
Come fully forth, let others see you
Who you are - you're special too

Author notes:
A writer should never be in hiding. His or her thoughts on
paper are scribed forever. Their own words make them an
open book for all to see, and taste; and of course - know.

Sister Ginny's Butterfly Bush
Garden Visitor
by Don G. Ford

Just when you thought the flowers

In your garden were so grand

Along comes something special

It flutters, floats, and lands.

All dressed in royal colors

Its bright array of wing

And as it lands on petals

It doesn't weigh a thing

Each daisy, rose and daffodil

Each time he chooses them

You hear the clap of leaves

And every flower bows its stem.

Who is this author?:

Don was invited to be a part of the National Library Campaign in 2011, "Create Your Own Story at the Library." This took place in April. The library covered the cost of the reception, since it was a National Campaign. See his first sold art piece >>>

His art was up for the entire month, and stories accompanied many of his pictures.

Dear Don,

It is my great pleasure to inform you that your poem "Each Flower Child" has been chosen for publication in the February issue of Four and Twenty Poetry, scheduled to release on Tuesday, February 15.

In just six days
He made this world
And every child
A flower in it

Don's reinventing himself these days as a Writer/Artist in his Storytelling adventures. I feel like he lived inside a book most of his life, and now he is finally coming out of it into the real world. He's hopeful everyone likes what they see and hear.

Don speaks at retirement homes and schools that invite him. This he has done since 2010. Once he walked into a convalescing home, and was greeted by a woman whom they say you should never give full eye contact to. She walked right up to him and took his hand. He knew he was in for a wild ride then. But what is a body to do? We may think that person is out of it, but they really are having an adventure in their own mind, and taking you with them. They are probably remembering a past event.

It was sad and charming rolled into one. He could not turn his back on this poor gal. She seemed so needy, and he was just there as a sounding board. For some folks, that's all they need; a little something to get them through a long cruel day.

If he can turn even one smile right side up, it's worth his trip.

Don G. Ford Books published thus far:

http://tinyurl.com/l4al233

Most of the books are a compilation of short stories, letters, writer tips and dialogue put together over the last eleven years.

Most of the art pieces in his books are photos that have been put through a digital process to fit the book or story line.

I Feel I've Known You Always

An invitation carries me,

As I head out in the wood.

The air all crisp and clean;

The walk will do me good,

Sometimes I skip and kick a stone,

Or moving on I'll stop and stare.

I'll look hard at a squirrel's nest

To watch for any movement there.

I'll study how they did it,

Without the duct tape or the glue.

The wind will blow and not disturb,

And all that I recall is true.

I hear the blue jay just ahead.

He is the eyes and ears for all.

He leads the wildlife, so it's said;

And sometimes sounds his trouble call.

The deer is color blind, I'm told;

But not the turkey in the tree.

He spies our movements from above.

He keeps his eyes on you and me.

Last of the Honey Bees

By D.G. Ford

Today was like every other day. It was always the same routine. Heading out to the pasture where the clover grows, I would draw my daily fill from the flowers there. But instead of the usual hum from all of the other bees, I felt somehow alone, separated from all the others who make their daily pilgrimage there too.

Something was very wrong. I was feeling closed in and didn't enjoy it one bit. It was like someone had turned off the lights. It was a warm day, but suddenly a cold and clammy feeling came over me. Was I going to die? I couldn't shake it. Another drink of nectar might have helped. Maybe my blood sugar was too low.

I was experiencing a bit of dizziness and it was not going away. Also there was no feeling in my left wing. I had to land. Things were beginning to blur. It was broad daylight out, and shadows were all I saw. I felt so weak. Then I felt like I was being lifted. I had no control.

"Bee, it's ok, it's me your keeper. I am putting you in a special case with a few of your friends."

"But where is all the rest of the hive?"

"There has been a mass destruction occurring over the entire bee population. Most of the hives have been killed off by a parasite or something. You are one of a few who seem to have been able to withstand the effects of this blight."

"But I was weak and lost the use of my left wing. I am still a bit dizzy also."

"I had to smoke you, so I could capture you. The smoke will wear off soon. I really need a blood sample for the Tox Lab. They think you may be the cure – that your genes are resistant to this epidemic."

"Fine, take all the blood you need. Glad to be of assistance."

DAYS LATER:

"Thanks for your help. The other bees are all doing fine. The Lab people liked what they saw in your blood culture. You have a strong strain of anti-toxins in your system that they believe over time will bring back the hives to their full potential."

"Well, that's good news. If you need me again, I'll BEE over in the clover."

Says the Butterfly: "We must all learn to crawl before we fly." D.G.FORD

There is a path marked for all. Some along the ground and others head for the sky. D.G.FORD

"The best things in life are free" Anon. - Butterflies are no exception. D.G.FORD

[Can we be counted on to help this fragile of all creatures in our world? We need one another.]

Kids out in the environment;
visiting things in nature.

Maybe kids could put away their electronic devices for a short time to catch a peek at nature and its various elements. If they have their phone along, it could be used only to capture pictures in the woods or along a trail or waterway.

[A Great Book For Science Classes Heading Out Into Nature On A Field Trip]
https://tsw.createspace.com/title/4838245

Want to know where you can donate to help the butterfly population? Here is a good starting place! See link below.

https://
savethemonarchbutterfly.wordpress.com

More books by Don G. Ford

If you missed Book 1, "A Story Runs Through It", it is found Here > > > >
https://www.createspace.com/5280532

Book 2 is now out and available.

Both books are a Patchwork of varied genre stories; something for almost anyone. Book 1 and Book 2 are each 30 Chapters long, in full color and cost more!

The direct link to Book 2 is here > https:// www.createspace.com/5330570
Cheers, Don

P.S. These are mostly tales plucked from my own life. Book 2 title is:
"A Story Runs Through It/Before The Ink Dries"

[ALONG WITH THE BIRDS AND THE BEES, YOU WILL BE SURE TO FIND MORE BUTTERFLY TALES IN THIS MIX TOO.]

OTHER Story Book Friends are found here also:

As a child, hadn't you ever thought,
I'd love to be that butterfly?
Moving from flower to flower
And soar to the top of the sky.

Flying
from
flower to
flower
and book
to book

To be captured in a book
Is maybe the best life for me
There I could live forever
On every page I'm set free

Butterflies come with spots and stripes
All manner of colors, a grand display
They never make a sound you see
They always arrive on golden rays

The sun comes out to dry the rain
So we hear folks often say
And butterflies will wait it out
As warm sun rays help them stay

On wings here comes a friend of mine
I could never ever eat a butterfly
Even if it looked like a cookie
Even if it meant I'd starve and die

I think a butterfly should get
A Junior Flying Ace Award
For the miles and miles he soars
He's never tired - he's never bored

Higher and higher flapped those tiny wings
They watched as birds and planes flew by
Each seemed to almost touch the sun
I think it's why butterflies fly so high

If Heaven is reserved for all living things
And if butterflies mind their Ps and Qs
A place in the sky is reserved for them
I'm convinced there'll be quite a few

The last word here >>>

The last word here >>>

An interesting LEGEND to end on.

An American Indian Legend

If anyone desires a wish to come true they must first
capture a butterfly and whisper that wish to it.

As a butterfly can make no sound, the butterfly can not reveal
the wish to anyone but the Great Spirit who hears and sees all.

In gratitude for giving the beautiful butterfly freedom,
the Great Spirit will always grant the wish.

So, according to legend, by making a wish and giving the
butterfly its freedom,
the wish will be taken to the heavens to be granted.

©www.Beadphoria.com

**We Need To Change the word Plight
back to Flight! See cover picture!**

I noticed a few of my books are headed off Amazon shelves. Maybe it's the approaching Holiday Season. Maybe folks are getting into the Spirit of Giving. Because my books are in varied genres there is something for everyone. Writing since the age of 15, I have covered many subjects areas, some based on my own real life experiences.

Because I'm a humor writer as well, I enjoy entertaining folks, and turning smiles right side up. I thought I would post the cover and a book description of each. **See if anything suits you!**

http://tinyurl.com/l4al233

Cave Land # War on the Home Front # A Story Runs Through It - Book 1 A Story Runs Through It Book 2 # PREVIEWS - New Children's Books # Clay Pond - What is a Woodie? # Came Thunder and the Rain # Connect the Dots # Think Poetry # Clay Pond and Other Fish Tails # Royal Ferdinand and Other Tales # Tree With the Money on it # Star at Christmas # Chilly The Very Warm-Blooded Polar Bear # Raising Hope # My Best Friend is a Leprechaun # Clay Pond - Big Black # Mirrored Self # Clay Pond - Lady Bugley # Clay Pond - We All Love Lacy # Nightfall Horror Anthology # A Nature Walk # Guess Who's Hiding at the Alphabet ZOO # Clay Pond - Freddie The Frog & Thaddeus Toad # Heaven on the Line # The Great Migration # Our School Will Never Be The Same # Funny Business # No Such Animal as Writer's Block # Floyd the Dog Story Book Commemorative

AND the latest book thus far: **What's all the Buzz About?**

https://tsw.createspace.com/title/8252721

www.ingramcontent.com/pod-product-compliance
Lightning Source LLC
Chambersburg PA
CBHW050833290526
45792CB00001B/377